# Overcoming Co-Dependency
## through the Elimination of Human Relations

# Overcoming Co-Dependency
## through the
# Elimination of Human Relations

### The mildly Depressed Person's Guide to Daily Living

Mona Lovejoy  Sunny Knight

Halfway House
1995

A Halfway House Publication

Copyright © April 1995
Donlu Thayer and Patricia Pélissié
The Lazarus Trust

Printed in the United States of America
All rights reserved

No part of this book may be used
or reproduced in any manner without the
written permission of the authors,
except in the case of brief quotations
in critical articles and reviews.

For inquiries, address
Halfway House Publications,
Post Office Box 242, Provo, Utah 84603.

FIRST PAPERBACK EDITION

*This book is lovingly dedicated
to you,
the Depressed and Downhearted Everywhere,
regardless of
Age, Sex, or Body Weight*

# Spurious Commentaries Concerning This Remarkable New Book

Albert Einstein: "A Universe of Truth."

Thomas Edison: "This book is about as useful for depression as the invention of the light bulb."

Franz Kafka: "It changed me into a completely different creature."

St. Augustine: "An impressive work of the spirit of self-recrimination, which was no doubt composed not by two soul-less fictitious women but by a single sublime man."

William Shakespeare: "The tongue which drippeth truth shall e're prevail; The pen which marks the page shall drive the nail."

Hamlet, Prince of Denmark: "If only my wretched mother had read this book!"

Wolfgang Amadeus Mozart: "Too many words."

Jean-Paul Sartre: "*L'enfer, c'est les autres.*"

Isadora Duncan: "Thin persons may also be depressed."

Julius Caesar: "Veni, Vidi, Rideri . . . dum Lamentari."

Socrates: "ἕτεροϱν τόδο ἦ οὔ;"

Sigmund Freud: "This book will set the course of Western Civilization back a hundred years."

The Baron Wilfried von Schnornhausen: "Dieses Buch ist von ein paar Verrückte geschreiben!"

Abraham Lincoln: "Mrs. Lincoln and I enjoyed it very much."

Blanche DuBois: "Don't let them take it away, Stanley!"

Alexander Graham Bell: "Listen. Is anybody listening?"

## About the Authors:

They are (mildly) **depressed**.

Consummate literary/musical Artistes and utterly dedicated houseperson/professionals who are just a teeny bit overweight, they have, between them, approximately 2 spouses and 11 children, as well as something approaching 100 years of experience in the Co-Dependent/**Depressive** Arena.

Their qualifications thus go without saying, and their particular biases are all too abundantly evident throughout this work.

## What the Authors Themselves Have to Say about the Title of this Book:

The term CO-DEPENDENCY is a modern, transitory word which is usually no longer hyphenated. We, however, like the looks of the word better when it is clearly divided, and, moreover, think that there is a certain metaphorical significance in the hyphenation process. Although we do not intend to be held to this opinion throughout the book.

Let us define the two parts of the term: First, CO, meaning *with* or *at the same time as*, and then DEPENDENCY, having to do with *a certain relationship of one person needing or counting on another*.

CO-DEPENDENCY thus means *people needing to be with or count on each other a very great deal.*

Obviously, this transitory Modern Term covers an enormous multitude of immutable Ancient Sins.

Some of these Sins otherwise might have names such as: unflagging friendship, undying love, pathological caretaking, symbiotic lust, sick obsession with one's abuser, sick obsession with one's victim, standing by one's man, hating the sin and living with the sinner, emotional martyrdom, strict disciplinarianism, indefatigable courtship, Relentless Whirlwind Romance, rapturous self-effacing philanthropy, and ADEQUATE SELF-ESTEEM (which is codependency with the SELF).

Many if not all of these things, coincidentally, have been known to be major contributing causes to the very prevalent psycho-physiological state commonly known as (mild) **Depression**.

(Mild) **Depression**, in its multiplicity of forms, both Overt and Covert, is currently rampant as well as rather trendy in The United States of America and Its Territories, and is, in turn, a leading cause of those twin dark threads of the American Social Fabric:

The time-honored afternoon television serial known for obscure and archaic reasons as the "Soap-Opera."

And the more recently invented, less fictitious albeit somewhat more sensational phenomenon--the Inadvertently Titillating Afternoon Talk Show.

But we digress.

(Mild) **Depression** is nothing more nor less than a Compression of the Affect (the way one feels about and relates to persons, places, and/or things; in other words, NOUNS). Such Compression leads to a certain Inelasticity in Interactive Response, a sort of Emotional Hardening of the Arteries, as it were.

This merely means that Mildly Depressed Persons are Situationally Inert. If moving, they tend to keep moving. If stopped, they fix upon the Nearest Noun.

Or, to choose an Automotive Metaphor:

Mildly Depressed Persons tend to be gear-jammed. Some stuck in low gear, some stuck in high. Some bucking from reverse to overdrive and back, no cruising in between. Some spinning their wheels, foot on the brake, gas pedal to the floor. Some "revving" in neutral. Some idling in park. In all events: No Passengers, Please.

Because, as Almost Everyone knows by now, whenever two people are in proximity, some kind of CO-DEPENDENCY is likely to break out at any moment. And the main thing with any kind of CO-DEPENDENCY is to get rid of it.

We have noticed that some success has been reached during the past few years in the effort to *just-let-the-word-die-out-of-the-language-by-itself.*

Still, however, the best way to Eliminate Co-Dependency from your life is to get rid of everyone in your life except yourself.

Hence, this Little Book. To help you make it through Yet Another Day.

# In Place of a Table of Contents

## Some Possible Chapter Titles, Some of Which May Be Found in This Book

1. So This Is Hell

2. Anxiety, the Codependent's *elan vital*

3. You and Your Endorphins

4. Cruising the Void

5. Over the Edge and Back Again

6. The Theobromine Alternative:
   The Spurious Etymology of *Chocolate*

14. Grooming, a Daily Crisis

7. Depression in Community: You Do Mine
   and I'll Do Yours. (Already, we know we are
   not doing this chapter.)

8. ~~Housework~~

9. To Sleep, Perchance to Dream

13. Blessed Chaos--The Esoterics of Time
    Management

17. Depressed Persons in History

# Chapter One
## Cruising the Void

Depressed Persons need two things:

(1) STIMULATION and/or SEDATION and

(2) ASSIGNMENTS.

Besides these, they need a few more things;

(3) LARGE PRINT and WIDE MARGINS, to let in the light.

(4) Also they need VALIDATION and hence

(5) FRIENDS WHO ARE ALSO DEPRESSED and therefore self-absorbed enough to endure the entertaining Pathological Confessing and Self-Recrimination inherent in the Depressed Personality. (See PARALLEL PLAY.)

NOTE: While such "Friendship" is important (see AVOID FREQUENT PLUNGES TO THE DEPTHS), it should not be confused with Actual Relationship. In Automotive Terms, such "Friends" are those who, having their own desperate grip on the Great Steering Wheel of Life, are not likely to attempt an invasion of anyone else's Passenger Seat. (See also DEMOLITION DERBY.)

Note also that, in seeking Validation, The Ordinary Depressed Person should take care to avoid those persons exhibiting the Therapeutic Personality (who are themselves at least mildly depressed, though they would never admit it).

Yes, indeed. You must beware of these apparently attentive persons who need Your Depression more than you do, who may easily be identified by such tedious feedback phrases as "*I hear you*" (delivered meaningfully) or "*What you are saying is . . .*" or, worst of all (delivered reassuringly), "*I understand.*"

Because NOBODY understands you, nobody knows your Hell, nobody sees or could ever see the fearsome, unfathomable depths of your Black, Incomprehensible Grief, the intensity of your Fierce, Unrelenting Pain, and the sooner your few remaining So-called Friends get this straight and stop pretending to try to *understand*, the better it will be for EVERYBODY!

Sorry.

## Chapter Two
### Depressed Discourse

Anyway, this book is intended to offer some Stimulating and/or Sedating Assignments, on pages with plenty of white space, which are designed to facilitate the utilization of Self-Validation, with or without, and perhaps even in place of, a (Non-Therapeutic) Friend.

Now, in admitting the important essentiality of the Eliminization of CO-DEPENDENCY, the Authors do not mean to suggest at the same time that it would be in any way particularly advantageous to eliminitize

𝔇epression 𝔦tself, which although perhaps caused partly by a CO-DEPENDENT TENDENCY, is, **in itself**, a useful, perhaps essential, *Coping Mechanism*, without which *Life* could be incomparably **worse**.

The purpose of this **Chapter**, as is 𝔅eautifully 𝔍llustrated in these few successive ¶aragraphs, is to explain how *mildly* **Depressed Persons** can benefit from *Verbal Doodling*.

A sort of Erratik Changing of *Verbal* FONTS, as it were, which keeps **Functional Persons** off balance, **The Outside World** at bay: The Clients impressed, **The Boss** intimidated, and The Nosy Neighbors on their own side of the 🄵🄴🄽🄲🄴!

One form of *Verbal Doodling* involves the manipulation of actual VERBS, rendering them as static as possible, in order to slow down the Inter-Communication Process so that a semblance of coherence might emerge through the Blessed Foggy Haze of the (mildly) Depressed Brain.

This may be accomplished, for instance, by the employment of a plentiful amount of *-ize/-ization* and *-ate/-ation* words. These are not real words, but rather are perfectly acceptable airy mangling of the English Language which gives an impression of mental acuity. Use/Utilitize them freely, and no one will suspect that your brain is (mildly) unwired. (In addition, making up such words can provide a harmless modicum of that Needful Stimulation and/or Sedation.)

Here are some examples: *facilitate, facilitization, prioritize, prioritate, utilize, utilate, relativize, verbalize, verbalate, socialize, socialate, idealate* (as opposed to mere "idolize"), *perimiterize, parentize, interiorize, exteriorize, ironize/ironization* (from "irony," definitely NOT "iron*ing*"), *initialize, finalate, compartmentalize, sanitate, maximate, regurgitize*. And so forth, *ad nauseam*.

Virtually any NOUN (any part of speech, really) can be turned into a Static Verb in this fashion. While ordinary verbs such as *do, help, order, decide, use, speak, enjoy, admire, take care of, surround,* and *vomit* can fairly evaporatize, with their force, simplicity and precision, that Blessed Foggy Haze.

Also, REPETITIOUSNESS and REDUNDANCY, are also distinguishing hallmarks of Mildly Depressed Verbal and/or Written Doodling Discourse, as are, in addition, EQUIVOCATION and/or WAFFLING.

(Well, YOU just try to do without *and/or* for a week or so, and then go have *your* blood-pressure checked!)

And, finally, when all is neither said nor done, there is always that famous good old reliable Depressed Person's Mental Circuit Breaker-- SUDDEN, UNACCOUNTABLE DIGRESSION.

FACE IT! Your life is full of too many people, too many commitments, too many problems. Too many rules. Too many decisions! Too many responsibilites. You have too much to do, and you are too tired!

FACE IT! Everything that happens is your responsibility, even earthquakes.

FACE IT! No one will ever understand you. No one will ever know your pain. This cannot be said too often.

# Chapter Three
## Making It through Another Day

Zzzzzzzzzzzzzzzzzzzzzz.

(Do not neglect to plug your ears, unplug the telephone, and tape the doorbell.)

(Also, remember to muzzle the guard-duck.)

## Little-known, Well-kept Secret:

All truly Creative Persons in their Right Minds savor Depression. (Depression being essentially, though not necessarily, a Right-Brained Activity.)

But, realizing this, it is important (no matter which side of the brain you favor) to Avoid Frequent Plunges to the Depths, where one might be tempted to, say, Self-Mutilization.

For, the prevalence these days, in most parts of the country, of Emergency Medical Personnel makes Medical Intervention in such cases well-nigh inevitable, resulting in a significant amount of Caretaking/Nurturing which, following upon a significant amount of Real Physical Suffering, could finish-off a carefully cultivated Depression.

THINK ON IT: Vincent Van Gogh, living in the 1990s, would have kept that ear and been put on Prozac! At what great loss to Western Civilization!

# Chapter Four
## Depression in the Workplace

Yes.

# Unknown Scientific Fact:

According to Hypothetical Ultra-Modern Chaos Theorists, your Depression, be it ever so faint as the fluttering of tiny butterfly wings, most surely, rhetorically speaking, affects not only the weather in Casablanca and the stock market in Tokyo, but also the political situation in the Persian Gulf and annual fashion fluctuations in Buenos Aires.

## Chapter Five
### CLINICAL Depression

Seriously now, as a Depressed Person, you must understand that your Condition, no matter what anyone else thinks, is not in your Head, but in your . . . Brain.

Depression, as is well known by the Knowledgeable, results from Chemical Imbalances and/or Other Traumas caused by Hereditary and/or Environmental Defects, and/or by the incessant necessity of Dealing with Others (see **BLAME**), which leads to Misrouting and Misprocessing of all information received by the Brain.

Truly speaking, Depressed Persons (no matter how mild) necessarily and beyond-their-control, see the world as if through mud-streaked glasses.

Hence, the extreme importance of Accurate and Timely and Particular Medical Diagnosis, by Qualified Impartial Mental Health Practitioners. This usually takes place in some sort of a CLINIC, and results, therefore, in a formal variation of the **Depressed State** known as CLINICAL DEPRESSION.

By comparing your condition with that of others known to be CLINICALLY DEPRESSED, you may feel free to call your **Depression** CLINICAL, even though you have not attended an actual CLINIC for the Accurate Impartial Timely Diagnostic Process.

Another useful term is **Certifiably Depressed**, though this may be less satisfying than CLINICALLY DEPRESSED, due to its unfortunate resonance with **Certifiably Insane**, which has come to be more of an Epithet than an Actual Diagnosis.

## Making the Most of BAD and other CLINICAL Conditions

If Bi-polar Affective Disorder (BAD), which used to be called Manic-Depression (MAD) (which is our term of choice, its having a much better *cachet* as it were) is your Official CLINICAL Diagnosis, make the most of it. Few persons outside the Officially and Accurately Diagnosed World of the Depressed, other than actors and other professionals of ill-repute, are given such license to the melodramatic.

Being MAD merely means that one has a Swing in one's Affect. (In Automotive Terminology, this is the Overdrive-Reverse-Overdrive Phenomenon. Hard on the transmission and the garage door, but very entertaining for the neighbors.)

MADness, like All Other CLINICAL Conditions, may be compounded during certain times of the year by Seasonal Affective Disorder (SADness), which is caused by clouds.

Perhaps this is why, earthquakes notwithstanding, there are very few Depressed Californians.

A good thing for a BAD/MAD/SAD Person to do (besides move to California) is to ferret out from among The Depressed Friends one who is similarly afflicted.

The two may then "swing" together, either in unison or in contrary motion. Or perhaps in some interesting variation of contrapuntal harmony or deeply satisfying dissonance. As, for instance, in a canon or round: *Row, Row, Row Your Boat Gently Down the Stream* begun willy-nilly, who cares who comes in where, etc.

Contrary Motion in Manic Mood Swings is nice, because it provides moments of Blessed Solitude when the Mutual Swings are on the "outs," contrasted with often-Stimulating Encounters, as the pendulums swing in, to blissful collision.

Should you happen to be a Musically Challenged Depressive (which is perfectly all right; the World needs Your Gifts, too; We Ourselves, though you will not be able to detect it here, are somewhat Automotively Challenged), these lovely Musical Metaphors may be incomprehensible to you. In this event, merely think of Monkeys Swinging on Vines, or Demolition Derbies, or move on to the next section.

BEWARE! Spouses who are both MAD should take particular care to avoid contrapuntal collisions. A Gavotte or Minuet or Country-Line-Dance metaphor might be more useful than, say, a Canon or Fugue metaphor.

(While the Eliminization of Human Relations is indeed a worthy goal, the Eliminization of Humanity in its Entirety could have rather unpleasant repercussions for us all. In other words, since you cannot ride together, one of you had better get off the road.)

Also recommended for the BAD/MAD marriage (especially in cloudy weather) are frequent total separations on the "out" cycles, with spousal communications limited to the telephone and/or facsimile machine.

Nobody writes letters anymore, so don't bother with that.

Unless you are some sort of *Victorian Throwback Depressive* 🌿♡🌿, and do write letters ✉, in longhand ✎ with nice pens (perfumed ink) on interesting paper resting upon mahogany desks beside vases of flowers 🌷 under swooping draperies, dressed in excessive amounts of flowing fabrics.

Just don't expect anybody to respond.

(Not that you *would*, accustomed as you are to taking neglect for granted.)

## The Multiple-Personality or Schizophrenic Alternative

For those Mildly Depressed Persons fortunate enough to be able to choose to recreationalize themselves in Mental Illnesses more profound than simple BAD/MAD, lessons can be learned from disorders involving the Multiplication of Identities (a crimson Jaguar yesterday, a beige Plymouth Caravan today, a simple Go-Cart tomorrow).

Multiplicity can be especially useful to those able to exploit their Depression into Literary Veins, writing novels, poems, and plays to bless the Universe and local Subterranean Coffee-houses with the deeply intoned Wisdom springing from their private and exquisite States.

In **Our Opinion**, CLINICALLY **Depressed** Certified Pathological Liars should most definitely consider exploiting their natural gifts in this fashion.

One lacking the necessary Word-Processing Skills to become a Writer in this modern world (the pen is not made which is mighty enough to bear the burden of the Modern Depressive Soul; except see *Victorian Throwback*) could profitably consider obtaining educational enhancements which would make possible at least an avocation in the Written Arts.

Also useful in this regard would be *Journalizing* (not to be confused with Journal*ism*, which is *not* a field for the Depressed).

Journalizing is simply the leaving behind of intensely fictionalized accounts of one's life for posterity. One merely uses one's Compressed Energy to compartmentalize the Interior Life and then to present it as one wishes. Turning one's Pen into a Pruning Hook, as it were. Which is even mightier, after all, than turning one's Plowshare into a Sword.

Did you happen to notice that passing bit about Depression involving a state of Compressed Energy? (Not that we actually expect you to pay attention. We, as Depressed Persons, never ask of Others that which we would not be able to ask of Ourselves.)

The Compression of Depression has resonance not only Automotive but also Grocerial. Think of those tense vacuum-packed yeast or de-caffeinated coffee packages that spew particles and expand flamboyantly when you cut them open.

[*Freeze-dried* is something else. We shall not, however, think of attempting here a discussion of **Compression** vs. **Repression**.]

We have noticed that Compression is especially noteworthy among the Rescue-Driven-Depressed.

But this is too painful to discuss.

## Discreet Simulations of the CLINICAL Conditions

A Mildly Depressed Person may carefully simulate a Schizophrenia or Multiple Personality Disorder (MPD) by peopling the brain with companions, charming or horrific as desired (the Invisible Passengers, so to speak), who utterly understand One and therefore can maximize One's Suffering Potential.

These may be "persons," even whole colonies of afflicted person-like beings of whom one is not aware. Or they may be familiar persons with whom one might conversationalize, rationalize, commiserize, or otherwize consort.

In choosing this option, however, you will want to take extreme care to avoid that delicate and complex state--CDMPD, or Co-Dependency with, between, or among your Multiples. Eliminitization in this case can be peculiarly catastrophic.

Additionally, if you must insist upon Self-Diagnosis and/or Self-Treatment of the CLINICAL CONDITIONS, you should be aware of the fact that in doing so you will undoubtedly fundamentally alter dramatically the CLINICAL Balance of Nature by disrupting gainful increase for Qualified Impartial Accurate Mental Health Practitioners and by overloading the already precariously balanced requirements of Irritating Therapeutic Friendships.

Moreover, the Entire Pharmaceutical Industry could furthermore be utterly compromised, in a Redundant, Accurate, and Untimely Fashion, which could cause Crop Blights, Extensive Brown-Outs, and the Unsettling of the National Debt, leading to Global Hysteria.

Proceed at your own risk.

# Chapter Six
## The Theobromine Alternative:
## The Spurious Etymology of *Chocolate*

It is an incontrovertible, undisputed, proven fact that *Chocolate* is the most beneficial and useful of all substances for the Mildly Depressed Person.

This is because *Chocolate* contains Chemicals which make the Brain think that it is in love. And *Love,* even for the Recovering/Severing CO-DEPENDENT, can be a good thing. As long as it does not involve Other People. (See CONFUSION IN THE GARAGE.)

The power of *Chocolate* is hinted in its modern scientific name: *Theobroma cacao*.

Now, just forget about the "cacao" part. It only means something like "dark brown beans."

Much more important is the operative term, "theobroma," involving *theo*, from the Greek θεός, meaning "from on high, exalted, godlike" and *bro*, descending from the Old English 𝔅𝔯𝔞𝔞, meaning "an embrace around the bosom region, involving the heart and other sensitive body parts." *Ma*, of course, is cognate with *m-m-m!* and *me!*

Hence, *Chocolate* is *"A delicious godlike embrace of me above all else."*

What else can do so much?

Thinking upon Global Hysteria, however, please be advised that a Sudden Inordinate Rush to Theobromine Relief could dangerously rearrange The Present World Order, centering an unwonted amount of Global Power in Brazil, the Ivory Coast, Brussels, and Hershey, PA.

Once again, we ask that you Proceed at Your Own Risk.

And a Particular Note of Warning to the Deprivation-Dependent Depressive: Please avoid this *pleasurable substance*!

Unless, of course, a consequent **obesity** might lead to a subsequent shunning by all those whom you, perversely enough, persist in desiring to attract (and achieve Social Recognition from) among The Thin and Functional and therefore inevitably **FAT**-Prejudicial.

# Chapter Six-B
## (Diet)

a. Ballooning.

b. Stop the Yo-Yo, I want to get off.

c. Obsessive-Compulsive Meal Planning.

d. Intention is the Better Part of Virtue, or The Approach-Avoidance Gustatory Spiral.

e. **L**et's Get Real for a moment (and actually start this **C**hapter):

If you are a Depressed Caretaker, responsible for preparing the meals in your household, you are always too tired or too distracted to fix dinner, and not interested in eating it anyway.

Perhaps this is because you are still rebounding from this (late) morning's *Theobroma* infusion.

Or perhaps the effects yet linger from the Emergency Lunch with a "Plunging" Acquaintance (why else would you treat yourself to lunch out?) in the pleasantly murky atmosphere of the All-You-Can-Eat-Buffet at the **Kama Sumptuous**, where you were momentarily revived by the medicinal properties of turmeric, ginger, cloves, curry, cinnamon, and zitar music, before crashing into **Nirvana** for the rest of the afternoon.

Certainly, whatever you have done with your day, be it dozing at your desk, fixating on your screen, cat-napping in the faculty lounge, sleep-faxing, tele-mumbling, ricocheting through rush-hour traffic, or wandering aimlessly between the washer and the dryer, you simply cannot face the Evening **Wrath** of the Hungry Hoards.

And so, this HELPFUL HINT:

Some time during the day when you have a moment, you might Cleave an Onion (itself a very satisfying process; see LATENT HOSTILITY) and throw it (nevermind peeling it) into a large pot, a crock pot if you are able to plan ahead, and leave it on simmer. If you have the energy, you may sautee the onion first, for extra aroma.

Possible garnishments: Italian Seasoning, bayleaf, boullion cubes (unwrapped or not). A head of garlic would be good.

(Sorry, but microwave ovens are not well suited to this sort of subterfuge.)

For a simulation of Dessert-in-Process, throw a little Cinnamon into another pot. The Hoards will be assaulted, upon arriving, with the olfactory promise of a Veritable Feast.

(Did we mention that you must remember to add a generous amount of WATER to your pots? [See EMERGENCY MEDICAL INTERVENTION.])

Now, if you really want to buy a Goodly Hunk of Time, you might make the supreme effort:

SET THE TABLE, with at least one eating utensil at each place. (Napkins would be astonishing evidence of your good intentions.)

To prevent untimely lid-lifting and other possible sabotage, you might turn on the nearest television (if for some reason someone has turned it off . . .) and then, with your Last Breath, open the cabinet to leave the Peanut Butter jar accidentally in plain sight, with the knife sticking up temptingly, a loaf of bread placed strategically near.

And, finally, make sure that the jam and milk are immediately accessible in the refrigerator.

What an effort!  But well worth it, we promise.

"Aha!" they will think, your Co-Dependents, upon arriving from a hard day in the Jungle.  "Just a little peanut butter while we wait for this delicious (sniff, sniff) meal!"

And they will be glad (whether you are snoozing at home or away or *en route*) that you are not there to see them sneaking off with their stacks of Guilty Sandwiches to watch the Accidentally Titillating Afternoon Television Programs.

Which will gradually slog through Syndicated Re-Runs and dissolve into Perky Prime-Time Sitcoms.

Congratulations! You have successfully negotiated another Critical 3:30-7:00 p.m. Period. And, if you are lucky, the "dinner" table is intact, still set, for tomorrow.

We certainly hope, by the way, that you will not have forgotten to hide the remaining sliver of the Marzipan Cake in the back of the refrigerator with the crisis-stash of *Chocolate* behind the moldy leftovers, where no one will bother to look for it, and you will burn more **midnight calories** trying to get to it.

How often this Cooking Ruse will foil your particular Co-Dependents depends upon the contents of your spice cabinet and Your Own Creativity. (Don't start DEPENDING upon US to do all of your thinking for you!)

When Pseudo-Cooking fails (and it will, because everything does), you can choose the lesser of two chaotic evils and flee (or remain away from, as the case may be) the Domestic Premises to the Marketplace during these hours when Real Shoppers are home doing Domestic Bliss.

The quick Dinner-Hour Excursion into the Perils of the Marketplace can be especially useful for the Terribly-Agoraphobic-Depressed (TADs), who need clear, quick, non-competitive paths to and through their All-too-frequently-Necessary Consumer Tasks.

Taking the time to make these paths clear in the mind before venturing forth might be well worth the excruciating effort this requires (for the Agoraphobic, even bringing the Marketplace into Mind is traumatic), as it might relieve a TAD of the inevitable clammy vertigo of the Shopping Necessity.

ATTENTION AGORAPHOBICS: Always carry an adequate supply of *Theobroma cacao* on your person when entering the Marketplace for any reason whatsoever. We have also found that the Shopping-Cart-cum-Walker is a useful substitute for the support of a Steering Wheel. (See OUT OF GAS, AND MILES TO GO BEFORE I SLEEP.)

And remember that NO Depressed Person should ever feel under any circumstances obligated (with or without Shopping-Cart Support) to attend such Marketplace Events as Grand Openings, Truckload Extravaganzas, or Fire, Red-Tag, and Liquidization Sales, whether they take place during the Dinner Hour or not! (Sometimes, a bargain is no bargain.)

Now, we do realize that if you happen to be a Domophobic (home-dreading) Excessive-Active Depressive (DEAD), or especially if you might be a Terminally-Over-Achieving Depressive (TOAD), this whole chapter has been revolting to you.

Of course, Such a Feeling is certainly Your Right and Privilege, and 𝒲𝑒 would not for any reason want to deny it to you.

So, all right, TOAD! Just go right ahead and plague the universe with your pathological needs for Structure, Schedules, Correct Accessories, and Shopping-till-Dropping!

Very well, DEAD! You may just keep on pretending that all of this revving, wheel-spinning, peeling-out, and high-speed driving-in-circles means that you really are accomplishing something and moreover are feeling just great.

As with Your Feelings, these obtuse Behaviors are certainly your Right-and-Privilege.

And yes, although we might be accused of having scant unwanted experience in these areas, we want you to know that, after all: ***We do understand.***

Anyway, actually . . . truth to tell, we . . . even *We*, sometimes wish we were DEAD.

*Sigh!* This is really a long chapter, ostensibly about diet, and we are just too tired to finish it.

Let's see. "You are what you eat." If *that* isn't depressing . . .

Please see our Work-in-Progress, I Wish I Were a Chocolate-Covered Cinnamon Stick!

**Cinnamon**, incidentally, has been scientifically proven to mitigate the harmful effects of refined sugar in the diet. Mentioning this provides us with a clever way of returning to the subject of this chapter before abandoning it entirely.

## Chapter . . . Seven?
### Coping with Daily Tasks--Circling the Field

It is well known that Depressed Persons (DPs, pronounced "DiPs") of all sorts think differently from Undepressed Persons (UPs) of any sort, and that the two groups approach Daily Tasks in completely differing manners.

It is also well known that DiPs and UPs bore one another and therefore should never mix, in public or in private. Much of our National Crime Problem could be resolved by a Society-Wide acceptance of, and ability to cope with, this fact.

Sadly, the Mixed DiP/UP Family has ever been a Societal Inevitability. Hence, the need in the Average American Home for Many Televisions, to forestall those nasty battles over The Harmlessly Depressed *Simpsons* vs. The Cynically UP Newscasters Reading the Accidentally Sensational Nightly News.

Speaking of News, thanks to the Recent Discovery that some 98.6% of Us All now come from Dysfunctional Families and are therefore entitled to Inner Victimhood and Outer Exoneration from Blame for All Anti-Social Behavior, it is only a matter of time until UPs all across the Land will realize their Right to Depression, and the Mixed D/UP Family will be driven to extinction.

(See Instant Light and Bliss!)

Meanwhile, speaking of Thought Processes: While the typical UP will tend to think in a linear, Greek-like fashion, using a great deal of logic (an unfortunate invention of the Greeks which still pervades, even drives Functional UP Society), the typical DiP will think in a lovely *circular*, rather more organic fashion, involving such complex communication techniques as circumlocution, circumvention, circulation, and circumnavigation.

True enough, this "cir" behavior may cross over into alarming, less attractive behaviors, such as High-Speed Erratic Changing of Conversational Lanes (as it were) without Appropriate Signals, also Just Plain Babbling, and other sorts of repetitiousness known in Professional Cir-cles as Perseveration (headbanging and whatnot).

Nevermind. Even Perseverational Excesses (PEs) serve the DiP, who must ever seek relief from UP-Obsession with Peace of Mind (and from CO-DEPENDENTS who should just leave well enough alone and go off and join Babble-Anon).

As a matter of fact, in the Benign Eliminating Relations realm, there is scarcely anything that is more effective than Perseverational Excess.

Too often, however, really satisfying PEs are thwarted by those nasty Accurate Impartial Medical Interveners.

That is to say, if an UP should happen upon a trifly Overextended DiP "checking out" on a hard cold floor in a dark room, staring blankly into space at some Metaphorical Noun, conversationalizing with Invisible Codependents, laughing hysterically for no apparent reason, or rocking in time to a Barely Audible Chant . . .

The Meddling UP-Passerby will inevitably intrude, breaking the mood, and Therapizing with Cheerful Platitudes while nervously awaiting the Timely White-Coated Intervening Persons with their unpleasant tidy restraining garments.

Now we are going to have some sort of a CLINICAL PROCESS on our hands, involving not only annoying Third-Party Scrutiny and Catastrophical Bio-Chemical Assault, but also Significant Fiduciary Exchange.

Not so in Ancient Times, when such behavior might have been considered Interesting, even Amusing, and the Depressed Person might find esteem, even status as the lovable **Court Jester**, or bliss as the *Village Idiot*.

𝔅ut, once again, to return to the realm of the Daily Task :

While the UP will take a direct tasking approach, to and through the necessary chores, the DiP, more creative, will tend to Circumnavigation and/or Perseveration.

Consider a common problem, a Dirty Bathroom.

The UP will do something direct, such as . . . clean it and move on to something else.

While the DiP will be more creative, perhaps installing dimmers, or lowering the wattage of the light bulbs or removing them altogether in favor of scented candles, having already provided windows with light-blocking shades nailed to the sills, and perhaps even supplying fresh flowers daily, or artificial ones permanently scented and virtually indistinguishable from the real thing. From time-to-time a swift application of disinfectant spray.

Eventually, when health and/or esthetics, and/or guilt from having spent the afternoon Lunching, Rescuing, and/or Confessing, a more dramatic gesture might be necessary: A quick slosh of soggy Clorox-infested bathtowels over the worst parts, followed by swift evacuation of the premises. (Nevermind those little white blotches on the clothing. Just think of them as this season's wardrobe upgrade.)

No, you Irritating UPs and List-Making TOADs! This is *not* more trouble than just cleaning the bathroom regularly, systematically in the first place. And we are under no obligation here to explain why (you wouldn't understand anyway).

  Excuse us. Someone is apparently in need.

As we might have been saying: In contrast to the Wildly Creative Behavior of the Ordinary Convoluted DiP (OCDP), the Perseveration-Dependent DiP (PDDP), being very symmetrical, will take a slightly different approach to the Daily Task, which at first blush bears dangerous resemblance to typical UP Behavior.

Do not be deceived! Perseveration is the key. The PDDP *will* clean the bathroom. Over and over again. Over and over and over and OVER AGAIN!! The sinks, the shower, the tub, the toilet, the mirror, the floor, the chrome, the baseboards, the ceiling, the fan. Wearing rubber gloves and using rags, brushes, steel wool, Q-tips, toothpicks, and any other tool which might fit into tight places. Lysol on the doorknob (all knobs) four or five times a day. (For, who knows what evils proliferate from moment-to-moment upon unattended surfaces! Or lurk in wastepaper baskets, waiting to shout their filth at unsuspecting innocents!)

Now, you might be wondering how the TOAD approaches the Bathroom Problem . . . .

Like the PDDP, the TOAD will straightaway clean the bathroom. (Of course! It's on the List!) And, as with the PDDP, the cleaning will be frenetic. But it will not involve Perseveration, since the TOAD is driven by the List, and must hasten through to the end, in order to check off

12. Bathroom ✓    and be on to
13. Polish Philodendrons ✓
14. Re-organize Linen Closet ✓
   14a. Color-Code Towels ✓
15. Complete Inventory of Garage Tools. ✓

Meanwhile, back in the bathroom . . .

The DEAD? A quick swish around the sink, a quick squirt of air-freshener, followed by guilt-free escape from the Domicile.

Now, if such Bathroom Behavior--Perseverational, Circumnavigational, or even Domophobical--is not enough to dispel the stereotype of the Depressed Person as a Lazy Bum, we don't know what *is*.

Depressed Persons are NOT Bums of any sort! Whether Convoluted (Fat) or Symmetrical (Thin), they are merely Exhausted and Emotionally Flat. Which is definitely what *We* are after writing this chapter.

# Chapter Eight

## The Depressed Parent

¶f you tend to worry about the effects of your Condition upon your children, don't.

Depressed Persons are often Arrested or Distracted Over-Achievers who, given sufficient directed energy, might hassle their offspring with their own lingering Unmet Expectations for Success in Life.

Depression, therefore, could actually save your children from the excessive amounts of attention with which you otherwise might see fit to bombard them. Indeed, Benign Neglect could be a true blessing in your children's lives!

However, if WORRY is a Basic Need for you, go ahead and do it. Because there probably is, after all, some way Your Depression actually is causing your children irreparable harm.

Yes. Perhaps your inattention could leave a child in Unspeakable Peril, the world being what it is these days: A dangerous, threatening, dark, evil Predatory Wilderness full of perverts (animate and inanimate), slashers and sidewalk-prone vehicles of every hue, and homework-eating stray dogs, and brain-eroding filth in every Medium--oral, aural, and visual. And teachers corrupted by low pay, student violence, hidden weapons, misguided social trends, and government intervention and/or neglect. (Not to mention those Indelible Wounds from Tetherball Trauma or Peer-Criticism over that fumble during the football game at recess!)

(There isn't enough Cinnamon in the universe to meet the need for mitigation here!)

# Chapter Nine
## Sleep

Depressed Persons (have we mentioned this?) need a great deal of Sleep. Drugged, dreamless sleep is best, because snakes and monsters and the chambers of hell can linger most disconcertingly throughout the day.

Sleeping drugs , however, can have unpleasant side-effects, and are, moreover, notoriously unreliable. A useful alternative is Short Periods of Sleep (preferably intermittent, 'round the clock in unexpected places and never lasting longer than 3.5 hours), which keep one from entering the REM State, when dreaming is most significant.

The effect of this regimen, after a time, is similar to the lovely "wired" feeling resulting from ingesting certain very harmful and addicting substances.

Why take those naughty expensive drugs when Sleep-Deprivation is available free of charge and without prescription?

Prolonged Sleep-Deprivation, need we mention, has the added benefit of rendering those days-long BIG SLEEP periods which all Depressed Persons need (and to which we all, even TOADs, inevitably must succumb) much much more satisfying.

WARNING: Very Prolonged Sleep-Deprivation may induce *Actual Psychosis*, which could in some persons, dangerously exacerbate the snakes-monsters-and-chambers-of-hell problem.

# Chapter Ten
## Stimulation and the Depressed Individual, "Individual" Being the Operative Word Here

Obviously, this could be the most important thing that you as a Depressed Person (or that the Co-Dependent[s] for whom you have purchased this book) will ever read.

Herewith, then, a Few Suggestions for some Safe Singular (no passengers, please) Stimulatory Activities, both Active and Passive, which have been proven to be particularly effective in the facilitization of The Elimination of Human Relations.

Feel Free to Sort, Shuffle, and Select as Such Serves your particular DiSorder:

**ACTIVE Safe Singular Stimulatory Activities** might include such harmless preoccupations as shopping, decorating, housecleaning, redecorating, yard-working, aerobic excercising, prioritizing, photocopying, business-lunching, think-tanking, conference-calling, executive-boarding, committee-meeting, flying in/flying out, driving (fast or slow), sportscar-ing, midlife cri-sing, jet-setting, motor-boating, swimming-pooling, fishing/hunting, shooting (balls and guns), facili-tating, res-cuing, en-abling, country clubbing, competitive sporting, women's retreating, male bonding, locker-rooming, personal grooming, pryomaniatizing, dog-walking, bungee jumping, treadmilling, obsessional grieving, psychoanalytizing, and so forth.

Now, if merely attempting to think of perusing the above list has put you in spin, fret not.

Perhaps the **PASSIVE Safe Singular Stimulatory Activities** Category is more to your taste.

This category includes "watching behaviors" of all sorts. Though, since all else pales beside the Power of Watching Television, nothing else is worth mentioning.

As we have previously hinted, Television has benefits for the Depressed Person too numerous to list. Its being not only the perfect companion, due to its inherent rhythmic-buzzing, static, non-combatative, non-judgmental, unresponsive nature. But also its being our most immediately accessible, reliable, and convincing contributizer to the sense that the Whole World These Days Is Full of Filthy Garbage and Tragic Stupidity.

But this is too depressing even for **Us**.

Let us here simply emphasize the importance of Television's Great Alienizing/Eliminizing Potential.

Not merely in The Varieties of Basic Watching Behavior: (Are audible laughter and mockery permitted during *Star Trek*, or is this Serious Business? . . . Are you watching that thing, or is it just keeping you company? . . . I *am* doing my homework! . . . We *did* eat dinner, don't you remember? During *Wrestlemania*.)

But also in Simple Preference-in-Programming: (*Masterpiece Theater* vs. *Rescue 911*. *Barney* vs. *The Nude Dating Game*. *The MacNeil/Lehrer Report* vs. *Rush Limbaugh Live*.)

Not to mention Daily-Viewing-Dose-Tolerance: (Are five hours per day enough? Are fifteen hours too much? As long as they are not consecutive?)

Obviously, Television Watching is an exceedingly Complex Depressive/Familial Issue and could be a whole book unto itself.

We shall resist the temptation, however.

Because something more urgent has come to our attention after all, á propos of Watching:

It is increasingly apparent that Society in General must needs be wary of a certain Passive S.S.S. Type, the Vicarious Codependent or Passive-Energy Eavesdropping Person (PEEP).

Now, we might expect such persons in Personality Cults, Lecture Halls, Live Shows, Underground Magazine Shops, and Fan Clubs.

But how many of us are sufficiently alert to PEEPs among Aloof Neighbors, Envious Associates, and Lawn Care Professionals? Because PEEPism can strike anywhere, at any time (see PARANOIA).

Yes, it is now believed that Virtually Anyone, under enough Stress, could become a Pathological Gawker. And, though it is relatively long-range, PEEP Abuse is exceptionally debilitating for both PEEPer and PEEPee.

Moving right along . . .

If you are yet somewhat interested in including Another Actual Person in your short-range Stimulatory Behavior, that is perfectly all right. Just don't call on *Us* to extricate you from your willful co-dependent tangle!

And be advised: The enjoyment/spontaneity potential here could lead you out of Depression prematurely, short-circuiting the Private Grieving Processes you have so carefully cultivated.

# Chapter Eleven
## Politics and Religion

Simply said, as concerns Politics and Religion, Depressed Persons should assiduously avoid the former and enthusiastically embrace the latter.

Think on it. Are you able to muster the energy for Political Correctness, for instance? Do you have the mental agility to keep up with the particulars of the growing numbers of ways it is possible to insult people? What if, during a Public Appearance, you should slip and call a Mid-Street Maintenance-Entrance a **Man**hole!

And can you keep your Tangled Web straight at all times? Probably not. Avoid Politics like the plague. You probably shouldn't even engage in Political Discussions.

Unless you are one of those perverse types who enjoys the Stimulization of a Good Fight and the Solace of Post-Battle Self-Recriminizations.

An exception to the Depressed Political Rule (and doesn't every rule have at least one exception?) can be found in the Chronically Redundant Egregious Evasive Extrovert Pathological person (CREEEP). CREEEPs, as has been noted by more than one Social Critic, are extraordinarily successful in Politics.

The rest of us DiPs do better to stick with the traditional and/or modern Comforts of Religion, the varieties of which exceed even the Categories of Depressed Persons.

Thanks to Television (and doesn't every Social Blot have at least one redeeming feature?) it is even possible to watch religion in the privacy of one's own home, where one can precisely control the lighting. (See Seasonal Affective Disorder.)

A Polite Warning, however: Actual Religious Conversion can be exceptionally damaging to the Depressed State. If you feel susceptible here, you might want stick to Politics after all.

# Chapter Twelve
## Qualify and Quantify

Take a moment now to take stock:

1. Just how Depressed are you?
2. How much more/less Depression could you bear?
3. What about those around you? How does your Depression compare with and/or How is it affected by that of Others?

Just relax and think for a moment before turning the page.

Are you, for instance, a CREEEP living with a PEEP?

Or are you perhaps a ReC (Recreational Confesser) without a SAIL (Sensitive Attentive/Indifferent Listener?)

Is your Significant Other a DEAD TOAD? (A particularly lethal combination. Just put one of *those* behind a steering wheel!)

Worse, are you Any Sort of a DiP Whatsoever, shackled to the proximity of an UP!--one of those inexorably cheerful persons who lack a basic senstivity to the Real World, which would depress anyone with half a brain, who suffer little in themselves and hence pass along their Rightful Portion of Suffering to others. One of those hopeless, hapless persons who should be exiled to a miniature golf course or atmosphere-controlled bridge game for the rest of their lives!

What do such persons know of the depth and breadth of Pain-Before-Memory? Of Hideous, Relentless Abuse? What do they know of Intra-Uterine Grief?!

(See RUNNING NAKED THROUGH THE STREETS.)

How much of Your Condition could be blamed on Cheerful UP Insensates! Probably a great deal!

**Blame**. A very important word. Make lists.

And remember this above all: Although much Depression is CHEMICAL and therefore No One's Fault, all Depression is SITUATIONAL, and therefore Everyone's Fault.

# Chapter Fourteen
## The Grooming Crisis

And now, we come to the most difficult part of making it through any day: The Beginning.

Namely, Is It Morning Already? Oh, Just Look at This Hair!

But first, What Shall We Wear Today?

Of course, this depends somewhat upon your Acronym.

But, be you a variant of OCDP, a subdivision of PDDP, a PEEP, a CREEEP, or a TOAD, the main thing with Depressed Grooming, as with every-depressed-thing-else, is to eliminate DECISIONS.

So then, a Professional Person of either gender (regardless of body construction) will want to stick to the predictable: The (generously cut) three-piece ensemble with understated Power Neckwear.

While the Beleaguered Houseperson (thanks, of course, to television commercials, shopping malls, and consumer catalogs) must struggle with a baffling array of Covering Choices:

For the "waisted" (female): Skin-tight jeans, tuck-in tops, belts, buttons, rufflies, jewelry. Neon spandex and clingy leggings under baggy sweaters. (How thin does one need to appear to be?)

For the Less Symmetrical: Loose sweats, fatigues, medical scrubs, re-designed parachutes.

Baggy sweaters over clingy (stretchy) leggings. (How thin can one make people think one is?)

If we have not yet covered the Costume Issue for your particular Acronym, Occupation, or Body Type, we beg your pardon as we proceed along our all-too-apparent biases.

Let us then Celebrate the Ultimate Costume for the Mildly Depressed Person of Indefinite Contour:

The loose, all-weather, medium-sleeved, calf-length T-shirt. No binding leggings. (Who cares anymore about what anyone thinks about one's weight?)

At any rate, the Basic T-Shirt Item easily can be dressed up, when necessary, with simple neck jewelry (beads or even pearls) of varying lengths. Please, no annoying bracelets, watches, or rings. Except that in certain Social Strata, the tennis bracelet is important, and earrings are useful, even essential, garnishment.

If you are unfortunate enough to find yourself in this Societal Niche, you might need to keep an assortment of Earrings handy for swift placement, as when answering the door . . . But why are you answering the door? . . . to the Functional or Functionaries roaming the neighborhood and attacking at will.  Or for rushing to the elementary school . . . Why did you answer the phone ? . . . to administer a decongestant or deliver forgotten sundries.

(Nevermind making any appearance whatsoever at the high school, earrings or not, unless you fancy passing your Depression into yet another generation.)

Anyway, as your codependents know only too well, the T-shirt can quite comfortably be worn 'round the clock, to sleep (briefly) in at any moment--on the sofa, in the chair, under the dining room table or the Grand Piano.  Even in bed.

And is especially handy for those post-midnight moments when the police arrive, interrupting your snooze in the laundry room (somewhere between the washer and the dryer--see WANDERING AIMLESSLY), to question you concerning some disturbance in the neighborhood because all the lights in your house are on and the guard-duck is berserk.

Somehow, we seem to have lost the train of thought here . . . .

Did we mention that clip-on is best, speaking of the earrings? Ease of application or removal. (If matching is uncertain, remain in profile.)

Socks, or no socks. That is a question.

Shoes. When absolutely required, slip-ons, of course. Thongs, scuffs, sturdy slippers, clogs. Broken-down sneakers (no laces!) or those old Capezio Flats. Matching is not essential as long as

Confidence is Projected.

The hair. Eliminate it, as an issue. By wearing it wet or in similitude thereof. Add a little excess moisture to the face, and anyone you might accidentally encounter will think you have been exercising all day and will flood with admiration.

The Aerobic Ruse also eliminates the Makeup Problem. (Earnestly-Exercising-People do not retain their eyeliner.)

This is an exhausting chapter.

One more thing is worth making the effort to mention, however:

A nice long full chic comfy coat (or cloak for the Dramatic) in a soil-neutral color is useful over the T-shirt, not only providing significant camouflage, and warmth in chilly weather, but serving as a ready sleeping bag.

(The police, awakening you at 02:43, will merely assume, especially if you have reflexively grabbed The Earrings, that you are on your way to Visit The Sick, and will apologize for the interruption, instead of heaping silent scorn upon you.)

Scarves are also useful. (Again, see ISADORA DUNCAN.) Long, short, warm, cool. Head, neck, waist, wool, silk, even polyester in a pinch.

Feather or fur boas as well, wearing which, one could even attend an evening at the Opera (a very Depressing Art Form) in the T-shirt and a cloak. (Optimally, the shoes in this case should bear a slight heel, and should match.)

Throwing aside our bias for a moment, we shall be brought to observe that even Thin, Discomfort-Dependent Depressed Persons could perhaps find the T-shirt Regimen gratifying, with the simple additions of Wide Tight Belt, high-buttoned starched Dickey with Brooch, and high, leg-gripping Leather Boots.

*Cross-dressing:* Sounds interesting, but not an acutal option. Stimulating, to be sure. But too much planning, too many accessories. And perfect makeup and hair are absolute musts.

# Chapter Fifteen
## So This Is Hell

And now that we have successfully begun Your Day, it is, SADly, time to conclude.

May we say that indeed it has been a privilege to suffer with you, regardless of your Acronymn. To contemplate the exquisite, rich, darksome intensity of your Mildly Depressed Existence.

While others are choosing to float in the humorless euphoria of Anti-Depressants, or to be trapped in the vast, bland, vacuous, cheery wasteland of the Worldwide Recovery Movement.

And now, before we leave you to your fate, we offer one more Stimulating Assignment.

We have called it the Ultimate Non-relational Metaphorical Eliminizing Trip (UNMET).

It is very simple, and can be accomplished in the privacy of your own home, without expense or special equipment.

Just sit quietly (or lie back) and Imagine.

It is a beautiful, cloud-less, day. High on a windy hill, all of your Co-Dependents--all Nouns, Verbs, and Acronyms, have gathered for a final farewell.

Imagine them all there, needing, whining, begging, manipulating, bravely coping. Flattering you and charming you back into your old enabling behaviors. Infuriating and impossible to ignore.

But we shall very soon meet your UNMET Needs.

Just watch them. They can't hurt you; they can't touch you. (They are merely Metaphors.)

Now, imagine a Great Big Hot-Air Balloon, descending gracefully upon the crest of the hill. Imagine its bright and cheery colors. Your Co-Dependents, every last one of them, are thrilled. They begin climbing into the basket of the balloon, each one of them carrying a commodious suitcase bearing his/her share of Your Pathological Attachment, Your Anxiety, Your Grief.

Go ahead. Just let them all go. There is room for Everyone. (MORE BALLOONS, PLEASE!) And they are having a great time. (You don't have to worry. The Agoraphobics have been placed carefully near the center. They won't even know they have left the ground.)

All right. All are aboard.

Now, Launch!

The Balloons are rising, gently rising. Lifting from the hill. Everyone is having a great time, waving goodbye. Grateful to you beyond measure for coming up with this Metaphor.

What a Trip! Up they go, into the blue, blue sky. Up, beyond the wispy clouds, through the hole in the Ozone Layer and out into the Vast Black Starry Empyrean. Bye, bye!

And you, below. Alone. At last, alone. They are all gone. All your Worries, all your Woes. All your Relations. Never to return.

Alone, at last!

How do you feel? We'll wait while you decide.

Have you decided? Are you comfortable without that old familiar Anxiety coursing through your veins? Without that Old Co-Dependent's High to drive you, that Old Co-Dependent's Low to sustain you in the Depressive Crash.

You are probably just fine. After all, you have what you want: For the rest of your days you shall be a Recovering Human Being. As long as you remain alone.

Just think! Never again need you fruitlessly vow, upon Pain of Relapse, to guard at every moment against the possibility of Unhealthful Relationship. Never again, even once for a small moment, will you be tempted to Manipulate, Over-React, Wallow, or Enable.

Not for you, a spot on that endless roll of Great Depressives in History, many of whom struggled throughout entire long lives to endure Relations!

Just consider them! The vast assemblage of Co-Workers, Co-Stars, Co-llectors, Co-eds, Co-ordinators, Co-ops. Co-Pilots, Co-llaborators, and . . . Co-Authors!

The Endless Corps of Unrequited Lovers, Doting Mothers, Proud Fathers, Symbiotic Spouses, Tedious In-laws, Sibling Rivals, Kissing Cousins, Feuding Extended Families!

Theatrical Troupes, Scout Troops, Sales Teams, Athletic Teams, Cleaning Teams, Teaching Teams. Logging Crews, Grounds Crews, Framing Crews, Rowing Crews, Wrecking Crews. Partners, Mid-level Managers, Sorority Sisters, Lodge Brothers, Board Members.

Yes, Battalions upon Battalions of CO-DEPENDENTS, marching through the Corridors of Time since before the Beginning of Recorded Recovery! Not for you. You've sent them . . . *Us!* all away.

And here we are in the Vast Beyond, Cruising the Void in the Hot-Air Balloons of your formerly Depressed Imagination!

And we are having a wonderful time! (No parking, please. And no one must leave the vehicle! The Void, after all, is No Joke.)

But . . . You look so small down there. So far away. So . . . alone. Are you sure you're all right? Is there anything you need? Anything we have neglected to tell you, do for you? Get from you?

Because, it appears that one of the TOADs has just invented jet-propulsion up here. And, though it is really wonderful cruising the edge of Irresponsible Nothingness like this, we could, if you needed us, find a way to Come Back!

That's it. We've decided. We're coming! Can you hear us? Can you see us? Hey! Somebody put this thing in Down!

Whew! That was close.

But here we are, together again. DiPs of every hue. Symmetrical, Convoluted, TOADs, DEADs, CREEEPs, PEEPs, ReCs, SAILs, and Therapizers! Co-Dependents all.

What a Trip!

Good to be home, though. Because, finally all CAPITAL LETTERS aside, wouldn't we all really rather be depressed?

All right, then!

Move over, Beethoven!

# Chapter Sixteen
## Beethoven

Another Cadence, another Resolution.

Of all the Depressed Composers in History, the Most Depressed was, without a doubt, that consummate Classical/Romantical Musical genius, Ludwig van Beethoven.

All other considerations of biography and composition aside, Beethoven's Depression is easily detected in The Perseverational Quality of his music.

Have not Countless Depressed Persons Everywhere found Profound Undemanding Non-Relational Comfort and even Friendship in the familiar three-note Rhythmic Perseveration of the *Sonata quasi una Fantasia*, alias "The Moonlight Sonata":

*DUM-dum-dum,* DUM-dum-dum, DUM-dum-dum, DUM-dum-dum; *DUM-dum-dum,* DUM-dum-dum, DUM-dum-dum, DUM-dum-dum; *DUM-dum-dum,* DUM-dum-dum, *DUM-dum-dum,* DUM-dum-dum; *DUM-dum-dum, DUM-dum-dum, DUM-dum-dum, DUM-dum-dum* . . .

As Beethoven himself said in composing this piece (which he perversely enough dedicated to the Contessa Guilietto Guicciardi, whoever she was, who probably didn't care a fig for him, but being named "Juliet" was undoubtedly herself Depressed):

"This sonata does not obey the rules. It expresses what I, Beethoven, feel, and I am free to do this as my genius directs me."

HEAR, HEAR! We could not have said it better Ourselves!

And if Countless Homebound Depressed Persons have thus reveled in the comfort of The Moonlight, so many of the DEAD (in all corners of the Globe) have been quickened by the relentless four-note jab of the famous "door-knocking" motif of the Famous First Movement of Beethoven's Famous Fifth Symphony:

*Da-ta-ta-**TAAAA!** Da-ta-ta-**TAAAA!** **Da**-ta-ta-ta, Da-ta-ta-ta, Da-ta-ta-**ta!** **Da**-ta-ta-**ta**, Da-ta-ta-**ta**, Da-ta-ta-**ta!** **Da**-ta-ta-taa-**ah!** **Da**-ta-ta-taa-**ah!** Da-ta-ta-**ta!** Ta! TAA!*

Yes! Countless Domophobics have probably been catapulted into the Marketplace by such means, without even stopping for their Earrings or Power Neckwear! (Though we have not taken Surveys to ascertain the actual Prevalence of Beethoven's-Fifth-Utilization among the DEAD.)

If Studies were made, they might show that Beethoven has something to offer even TOADs, in his more hysterical compositions, written when Ludwig or some of his Multiples was/were on the "outswing" (see MAD).

A most noteworthy example might be found in the Variations and Multiple Cadences of the *Finale* of the Third ("Eroica") Symphony, the themes of which, having spent some ten years in that Magnificent Depressed Brain (having partially succeeded three times in sneaking out in other Compositions) provide the relentless, repetitious intensity precisely suited to TOAD Energy:

Namely, "Here we go again, when is this thing going to END?"

(See BATHROOM BEHAVIOR.)

Please! If there is a PEEP in your life, lock up the Beethoven! (Hiding it won't be enough!)

Speaking of When is this thing going to End . . .

$V_7 - I.$

# Chapter Seventeen
## An Appendix

Herewith, by Popular Request, a short list of Depressed Persons in History:

    The gods and goddesses of the Greek and Roman Pantheons
    Attila the Hun
    Genghis Khan
    Hannibal
    Napoleon Bonaparte
    Barbarian Conquerors in general
    The Conquered in general

Dostoevsky and Tolstoy
Russians in general
The Polish
Central Europeans
The Scots
Celts in general
British Islanders in fact (see SAD)
Kierkegaard and Nietzsche
Philosophers in general
Florence Nightingale
Lady Godiva (see RIDING NAKED
　　THROUGH THE STREETS)
Cleopatra
Her Admirers, and Italians in general
The Spurious Endorsers of This Book
Academics
Artists, Actors, Models
Novelists, Poets, and Playwrights
Musicians (with the exception of Coloratura Sopranos)
Independent Film-Makers and Their Families
The Self-Employed in general
Trekkies of All Generations
Baby Boomers
Inner Children
Therapists

Theologians, Clergymen, Social Workers
Health-Care Professionals in general
Corporate Executives
Publishers
Aristocrats
Peasants
Upholsterers
Mechanics
Lawn-Care Professionals
Sanitation Engineers, definitely
Women
Even gracefully aging Danish ex-playboy-millionaires may be depressed.

P.S.   Time Marches On.   So Can You.

*Love,*
         Mona & Sunny.

(See you Next Time!)

# A Table of Sequels
## Potential Forthcoming Titles from Lovejoy and Knight

1. **Our Friend, the Fat Molecule**

4. Lovejoy and Knight Take a Good Hard Look at Hyper-Activity

5. The Origins of Romance in an 11th-Century Southern French Religious Heresy

6. Armageddon, the Microchip, and You

8. ?

## And the Musical Sequels:

2. The Tempi of Obsession—*Molto Allegro* through *Troppo Prestississimo*

3. Anxiety and the Law of Octaves (Getting by, *do* to *do*)

7. Winding Down: *Plainchant* vs. Prozac

One more thing, in case your French, LATIN, γρεεκ, and German are a bit rusty these days (and whose isn't?):

We are certain that those of our Spurious Endorsers who perversely insisted upon their Native Tongues would want you, after all, to know their thoughts.

Mr. Sartre was beautifully empathetic: "It is very true. Hell *is* Other People."

While Mr. Caesar was deeply moved: "I came, I saw, I laughed . . . until I cried."

Mr. Socrates, surprisingly, seemed a trifle confused: "Is this something completely different, or not?"

While Mr. the Baron undertook somewhat to qualify his praise: "This Book was by a couple of Madwomen written!"